Meeting basic needs

Meeting basic needs

Strategies for eradicating mass poverty and unemployment

Conclusions of the World Employment
Conference 1976

International Labour Office   Geneva

ISBN 92-2-101675-7

First published 1977

ILO publications can be obtained through major booksellers or ILO local offices in many countries, or direct from ILO Publications, International Labour Office, CH-1211 Geneva 22, Switzerland. A catalogue or list of new publications will be sent free of charge from the above address.

Printed by Imprimeries Populaires, Geneva, Switzerland

Preface

As we enter the last quarter of the 20th century, and in spite of the immense efforts that have been made both at the national and international levels, a significant proportion of mankind continues to eke out an existence in the most abject conditions of material deprivation.

More than 700 million people live in acute poverty and are destitute. At least 460 million persons were estimated to suffer from a severe degree of protein-energy malnutrition even before the recent food crisis. Scores of millions live constantly under a threat of starvation. Countless millions suffer from debilitating diseases of various sorts and lack access to the most basic medical services. The squalor of urban slums is too well known to need further emphasis. The number of illiterate adults has been estimated to have grown from 700 million in 1960 to 760 million towards 1970. The tragic waste of human resources in the Third World is symbolised by nearly 300 million persons unemployed or underemployed in the mid-1970s.

The situation portrayed—however inadequately—by these figures has persisted, or even in some respects worsened, over the years, despite impressive rates of growth in many developing countries. Sharp inequalities in the distribution of income and wealth within and between countries have only served to highlight the depths of impoverishment of large sections of mankind.

Productive employment opportunities must be found not only for the approximately 300 million people at present unemployed or inadequately employed, but for a total of 1,000 million if those who will be entering the employment markets of the Third World over the next 25 years are included. The pressure on natural resources, including land, and on the environment will further intensify and may constitute additional obstacles to economic growth.

It therefore seems clear that major efforts will be required and major changes will need to be made in national development strategies and in the international economy if the world employment situation is to be improved within a generation and a substantial amelioration brought about in the standards of living of the working masses.

It was in view of the seriousness of the world employment situation, and the need to take corrective measures at the national and international levels, that the 59th Session of the International Labour Conference, held in Geneva in June 1974, adopted unanimously a resolution concerning the convocation by the ILO of a Tripartite World Conference on Employment, Income Distribution and Social Progress, and the International Division of Labour.

This conference, known for shortness' sake as the World Employment Conference, was held in Geneva from 4 to 17 June 1976. It was attented by tripartite delegations of government, employer and worker representatives from 121 member States. Government delegates included 70 Ministers representing not only ministries of labour but also other ministries such as planning, employment, trade, foreign affairs and development assistance. In addition, 22 official international organisations, 58 non-government international organisations and three liberation movements were represented.

Among all the words uttered by more than 200 speakers who addressed the plenary sitting of the World Employment Conference, one word stood out: *change*. Many different and sometimes conflicting views were expressed from the rostrum. But none of the 1,350 delegates and advisers voiced any doubts at any moment that the world must change its ways if poverty and unemployment are to be eradicated or greatly reduced by the year 2000.

The outcome of this world debate was the adoption by acclamation of a *Declaration of Principles and a Programme of Action* to effect major changes, both at national and international levels, in development strategies.

At its November 1976 session the ILO Governing Body authorised me to transmit the Declaration of Principles and Programme of Action to the ILO's tripartite constituents in member States, to non-governmental organisations, and to the UN Secretary-General and executive heads of other international organisations concerned, drawing attention to those recommendations contained in the document which call for action at the national level or, as appropriate, at the international level.

The purpose of the present booklet is to make the Declaration of Principles and Programme of Action available to an audience wider than that which will be reached by the formal act of transmitting the document to the parties mentioned above, and to summarise the objectives of the Conference, the technical and political preparation which preceded it, the general thrust of debate which took place in June 1976 and the main results of the Conference. This volume therefore reproduces:

(a) an article which appeared in the November-December 1976 issue of the *International Labour Review* summarising the preparatory work, the discussions which took place in the Conference, and the main results of the Conference; and

(b) the Declaration of Principles and Programme of Action as adopted by the Conference and endorsed by the ILO Governing Body.

Readers who wish to know more about the Conference may consult my Report to the Conference entitled *Employment, growth and basic needs: a one-world problem.*

December 1976

Francis Blanchard
Director-General

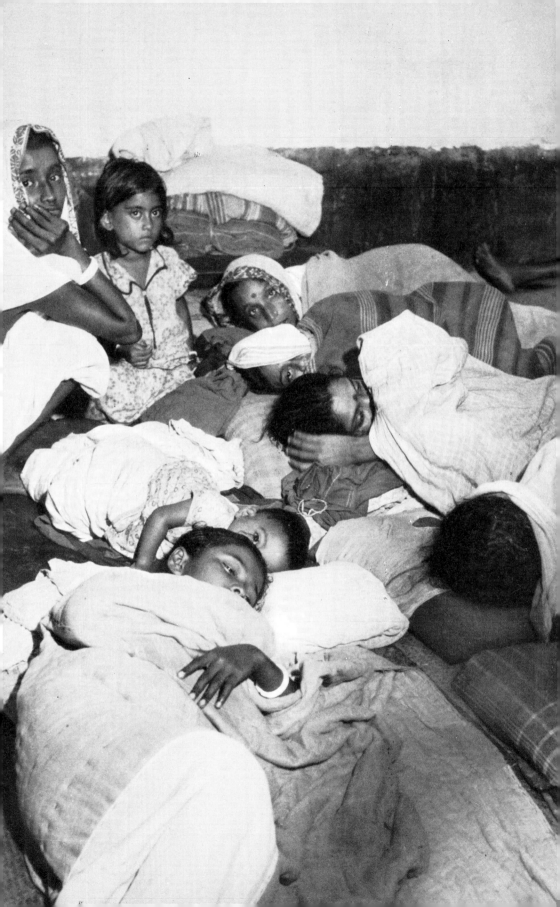

The World Employment Conference: a preliminary assessment

Louis EMMERIJ [1] and Dharam GHAI [2]

Introduction

The Tripartite World Conference on Employment, Income Distribution and Social Progress, and the International Division of Labour was convened in Geneva from 4 to 17 June 1976, in response to a resolution adopted by the 59th (June 1974) Session of the International Labour Conference. The resolution reflected a widespread concern with the gravity of the employment and poverty situation in the majority of developing countries, the threat of large-scale unemployment in several industrialised countries and the growing structural imbalances in the world economy. The Conference must be seen in the light of the series of world conferences that have been held in recent years to seek global solutions to global problems through discussion and negotiation. These conferences have provided forums for the discussion of environmental and habitat problems, population policies, the food crisis, industrialisation and trade prospects and policies, the law of the sea, the status of women, and a new international economic order. It was hoped that the World Employment Conference would propose national and international strategies and measures for a direct and concerted attack on the problems of poverty, unemployment and income inequalities. Since these problems are intimately related to the entire pattern of national and international development, the World Employment Conference touched in one way or another on the whole range of issues debated in the earlier conferences. At the same time, it was necessary to build upon the results already achieved elsewhere, to highlight the central problems of poverty and employment, and to focus more directly on the areas of competence in which the International Labour Organisation could make a contribution.

---

[1] Assistant Secretary-General, World Employment Conference.

[2] International Labour Office; Chief, Technical Secretariat, World Employment Conference.

It was in the light of these considerations that the Governing Body of the ILO decided on the following agenda for the Conference:

1. National employment strategies and policies with particular reference to developing countries.
2. International manpower movements and employment.
3. Technologies for productive employment creation in developing countries.
4. The role of multinational enterprises in employment creation in the developing countries.
5. Active manpower policies and adjustment assistance in developed countries.

Four distinctive features of the World Employment Conference should be noted. In the first place, it brought together representatives not only of governments but also of workers' and employers' organisations throughout the world. Secondly, it was concerned with both national and international dimensions of the problems of employment, poverty and international division of labour. Thirdly, it addressed itself not only to problems in the developing countries but also to employment and connected issues in the market economy and socialist developed countries, especially in so far as they relate to an improved international division of labour. Fourthly, the Conference itself was preceded by an intensive and somewhat novel preparatory phase.

The preparatory phase

The preparatory arrangements for the Conference were dictated by two important considerations—the severe limitation on resources available, and the lack of a formal mechanism for a continuing dialogue and interaction with the potential participants throughout this initial phase. Within these constraints the pre-Conference preparatory arrangements were designed to achieve three main objectives. These were to provoke world-wide interest, debate and engagement in the themes before the Conference, to seek in advance the views and advice of the tripartite constituency of the ILO as well as of the broader international community on the approach to be taken on the agenda items, and finally to secure maximum consensus on the proposals that might be put before the Conference for deliberation and decision. In all these respects the results achieved during the preparatory phase can be considered highly satisfactory.

The first stage in the preparatory process was the production of a draft document which, in its final form, would be submitted to the Conference as the Director-General's report. It was decided at an early stage that, in view of the interdependence of various agenda items, there should be only one comprehensive but concise document. Furthermore, it was considered important that the draft document should be prepared as early as possible in order to give adequate time for consultations and discussions prior to the drawing up of the final Conference report. Consequently the draft document, entitled *Employment, growth and basic needs: development strategies in three worlds*, was issued in August 1975. In the preparation of this document the Conference Secretariat received guidance from the Advisory Panel which had been set up by the Director-General and comprised distinguished development specialists drawn from universities, governments, trade unions and employers' organisations. The Secretariat also had extensive consultations with other outstanding experts from various parts of the world.

The second stage consisted of world-wide discussions and comments on the draft document. The document was discussed, among others, by the Advisory Panel and an Inter-Agency Working Party in August 1975. The Director-General invited governments, trade unions and employers' organisations to send their written comments by 1 December 1975. Senior officials of the ILO visited more than half of the ILO's member States to discuss the draft report and to solicit their support for the Conference. The response was gratifying. The draft document provoked considerable interest and discussion in various parts of the world, and the Office received extensive, detailed and sometimes critical comments from member States, trade unions and employers' organisations. The comments and suggestions received were carefully analysed and taken into account in the preparation of the final draft of the report the Director-General submitted to the Conference under the title *Employment, growth and basic needs : a one-world problem*.

The third stage consisted of a series of regional and group meetings prior to the Conference during the period from March to May 1976. The purpose of these meetings was to facilitate the emergence of regional and group positions on proposals made in the Director-General's report and to elaborate specific action programmes for presentation to the Conference. These meetings were convened by and at the initiative of the regional and group bodies concerned. The United Nations Economic Commissions for Asia and the Pacific, Latin America, and Africa and West Asia, acting in response to a resolution adopted by the Economic and Social Council in July 1975, convened preparatory regional meetings in Bangkok, Cartagena and Tunis respectively. Other regional groupings such as the European Economic Community, the Nordic countries, the Council for Mutual Economic Assistance and the Association of South East Asian Nations organised more or less formal consultations to arrive at common positions with respect to the themes before the Conference. Likewise various workers' and employers' groups arranged preparatory workshops. These meetings made a material contribution to the subsequent achievement of consensus at the Conference.

The expectations

It was hoped that in addition to stimulating debate on the vital issues of poverty, employment and income distribution, the Conference would be able to reach agreement on the broad outlines of national and international measures

A reasonable balance between labour-intensive and capital-intensive techniques ▷

needed to achieve objectives in these fields and on a number of concrete proposals advanced in the Director-General's report.

The single most important idea put forward in the report was that the focus of economic and social development policies should be shifted towards meeting the basic needs of the masses. The report spelt out in broad terms the major redirections of development policy required under a basic-needs approach. It was hoped that the Conference would endorse both the new emphasis on basic needs as well as its major implications for development policy. While this approach would need to be accepted and implemented at the national level, it was felt that the Conference's support could also help to make it the core of the international development strategy for the Third Development Decade.

In the field of adjustment assistance (i.e. measures to cushion the negative social effects of trade expansion) the report laid stress on the need to move from a passive, ex-post and piecemeal approach to an active, anticipatory and comprehensive one. Among the measures proposed to speed up the process of structural change in the industrialised countries, the report supported the establishment of an international reconversion fund. It was pointed out that the ILO Industrial Committees could play an active role in promoting adjustment assistance policies. The European socialist countries were urged to step up their imports, especially of the labour-intensive variety, from developing countries, in order both to stimulate employment expansion in the latter and to ease labour scarcities in the former.

On international movements of manpower, the report suggested a series of measures to enhance the welfare of migrants and to ensure a fairer distribution of benefits to the sending countries. It proposed that large-scale movements of persons should be governed by bilateral and multilateral agreements incorporating provisions to achieve these objectives. In the long run the preferable alternative was to promote flows of capital and know-how to take jobs to the workers. The report further urged adjustment of policies in both the developing and the developed countries to stem the loss of trained manpower from the former to the latter.

On the subject of technology, the report made proposals for the co-ordination and stimulation of research on technologies and products which have the greatest potential for improving the welfare, employment and incomes of poverty groups. It also addressed itself to measures designed to improve the flow of information and the dissemination of research findings relating to appropriate technologies and products. Two specific proposals were made: to establish a Consultative Group on Appropriate Technology and an International Appropriate Technology Unit.

On multinational enterprises, the report indicated various ways in which such enterprises could contribute to the implementation of a basic-needs strategy and to the achievement of a more balanced pattern of world production. It laid particular stress on the role that multinational enterprises could play in technological and product innovation geared to meeting the needs of the ordinary people. At the same time the report underlined the key importance of the host country environment in determining the amount and distribution of gains from the operation of such enterprises. In this connection it emphasised the need to enhance the bargaining power of developing countries in their dealings with multinationals.

The deliberations

The Conference brought together Government, Workers' and Employers' delegates from 121 countries, as well as representatives of 22 international organisations and 58 non-governmental bodies. In contrast to normal practice at the International Labour Conference, the Government delegates to the World Employment Conference came not only from ministries of labour but also from other ministries such as those concerned with economic planning, employment, trade, foreign affairs and development assistance.

Deliberations at the Conference were conducted at three levels. In the Plenary sittings the heads of delegation presented their views in general terms on the themes before the Conference. The Committee of the Whole, which was created by the Plenary, was given the mandate to discuss and negotiate the draft end product of the Conference and therefore had before it all five agenda items. It met in the first place for three days before breaking up into Working Groups. This provided an opportunity for the delegates to present their views on the various agenda items in more detail, with particular emphasis on the proposals that might be adopted by the Conference. It was at this stage that the results of the regional and group preparatory meetings were fed into the Conference deliberations. A number of government groups and workers' and employers' organisations submitted position papers on a declaration of principles and action programmes under different agenda items. Although there was inevitably some overlap and repetition in the speeches made in the Plenary and the Committee of the Whole, the latter was able to go into greater detail on the specifics of a possible action programme. The views presented in the Committee of the Whole provided important guidelines for the Working Groups.

Four Working Groups were set up to deal with the agenda items before the Conference, the second and fifth items—international manpower movements, and active manpower policies and adjustment assistance in developed countries—being taken together. The Working Groups were to report back to the Committee of the Whole. This procedure differed from that normally applied in the International Labour Conference, where the various committees report directly to the Plenary. It was, however, dictated by the interdependent nature of the agenda items. Just as there was one report dealing in a comprehensive manner with all the agenda items, it was necessary to have one Committee of the Whole to ensure that the reports of the different Working Groups would be fused into a consistent whole.

The crucial task before the Committee of the Whole, then, was to resolve differences among various groups and countries and to integrate the individual reports from the Working Groups into a coherent end product. The formula used was to set up a small group of people—" friends of the Chairman "—representing the Workers' and Employers' groups and several groups of governments. It took two long night meetings and two successive drafts to hammer out a report that could be accepted—not without a certain number of reservations—by the Committee of the Whole.

The contributions made by delegates to the debate at these three levels brought new insights and perspectives to bear on the themes before the Conference. This is not the place for a summary of the observations made by the spokesmen of various groups and countries. Nevertheless, it may be useful to provide a brief résumé of some major strands of thought expressed at the Conference.

Representatives of a few industrialised market economy countries and some Employers' delegates felt that the report overemphasised structural change and redistribution as essential requirements for a strategy to create productive employment and meet basic needs. They considered that the report did not adequately emphasise rapid economic growth, which they saw as the most effective remedy for social problems. Since this view was shared by a number of other delegates, it is necessary to point out that the report took the position that a considerable acceleration in economic growth over the rates achieved in the past decade and a half will be required to meet basic-needs targets within a generation, but that it is even more important to shift the pattern of growth in a direction which will immediately and directly benefit the poorer classes. Several delegates, most notably those from the socialist countries, argued that fundamental reforms in socio-economic structure were an essential prerequisite for the attainment of full employment and the satisfaction of basic needs.

Delegates from some market industrialised countries and several developing countries in south and south-east Asia believed that the report did not adequately stress the obstacles to development posed by rapid population growth. Other delegates, however, saw population growth essentially as a function of the type of development strategy pursued.

On the question of technology, Government delegates from many developing and socialist industrialised countries and several Workers' delegates felt that the report put too much emphasis on labour-intensive techniques of production in developing countries and that this would perpetuate the technological gap and continued dependence on developed countries. Here again, it is necessary to point out that the report did not advocate any extremist version of an international division of labour under which all labour-intensive activities would be transferred to developing countries while capital-intensive industries would remain the exclusive preserve of the industrialised countries. What the report proposed was a better balance in developing countries between labour- and capital-intensive technologies, which would generally imply higher labour intensity than hitherto in the modern sector but a more capitalised mode of production in the traditional agricultural and urban informal sectors, which after all include the majority of the labour force in most developing countries.

There was a significant divergence of views among participants on the responsibility of international economic forces for the persistence of unemployment and underdevelopment in the Third World. Representatives of most developing and socialist developed countries and many Workers' delegates traced the roots of the problem to the functioning of the international economy, while representatives of the market industrialised countries and the Employers' group tended to stress national factors and the need to take corrective measures at the national level.

It was, however, the subject of multinational enterprises that produced the sharpest differences of opinion. The discussions in the Working Group on Multinationals were invariably lively and often passionate. On the whole, Government delegates from the developing countries and the Workers' representatives wanted the Conference to urge strong checks and controls on the activities of multinational enterprises and to subject them to a legally binding code of conduct containing provisions relating, inter alia, to employment, wages, working conditions, reinvestment of profits and non-interference in the internal affairs of the host countries. Most of the Employers' spokesmen and Government delegates from several market industrialised countries, on the other hand, wanted the discussions to be confined to employment issues and were opposed to any legally binding code of conduct.

The outcome

The conclusions of the World Employment Conference are contained in the Declaration of Principles and the Programme of Action adopted at the final Plenary sitting.

The Conference endorsed the *basic-needs approach* to development in the following words: " Strategies and national development plans and policies should include explicitly as a priority objective the promotion of employment and the satisfaction of the basic needs of each country's population." It also adopted the major policy implications, at the national level, of meeting basic-needs objectives as set out in the report. The Programme of Action states that " basic needs cannot be achieved [in developing countries] without both acceleration in their economic growth and measures aimed at changing the pattern of growth and access to the use of productive resources by the lowest income groups ". It goes on to say that " often these measures will require a transformation of social structures, including an initial redistribution of assets, especially land, with adequate and timely compensation ". Furthermore, the Programme of Action puts emphasis on the participation of the people, through organisations of their own choice, in making the decisions which affect them, on developing inter-regional trade to promote collective self-reliance, and on a planned increase in investments. In the field of employment policy, " member States should place prime emphasis on the generation of employment, in particular to meet the challenge of creating sufficient jobs in developing countries by the year 2000 . . . ". With respect to rural sector policies, it is stated that " in view of the highly hierarchical social and economic structure of agrarian societies in some developing countries, measures of redistributive justice are likely to be thwarted unless backed by organisations of rural workers ". The Programme of Action also contains a special section on women, which recommends among other things " that the work burden and drudgery of women be relieved by improving their working and living conditions and by providing more resources for investment in favour of women in rural areas ". On population, it observes that " it is only through the fulfilment of [basic] needs, with special emphasis on the development of the position and status of women, that couples will be in a better position to determine the size of their family in a manner compatible with the aims of their society ".

The Programme of Action stresses the importance of international economic reforms and co-operation to reinforce action taken at the national level. Thus it declares that " the satisfaction of basic needs is a national endeavour, but its success depends crucially upon strengthening world peace and disarmament and the establishment of a New International Economic Order ". Furthermore, " the Conference recognises that the basic-needs strategy is only the first phase of the redistributive global growth process ".

A series of important recommendations concerning the basic-needs approach are addressed to the ILO and other United Nations agencies. Member States are requested to supply the ILO with their own definition and evaluation of basic needs and with a description of policies, existing and in preparation, to implement a basic-needs strategy. The ILO, for its part, should prepare before the end of the decade a report for a session of the International Labour Conference based on the replies of member countries.

The Programme of Action further proposes that the basic-needs approach should become an essential part of the United Nations Second Development Decade strategy and form the core of the Third Development Decade strategy. In order to ensure that a coherent United Nations effort is made to switch to a basic-needs development strategy it requests the Administrative Committee on Co-ordination to review, monitor and report on the work of the different agencies and regional Commissions of the United Nations system. Finally, it recommends that part of the $1,000 million International Fund for Agricultural Development be set aside for employment generation in the rural sector.

On *international manpower movements*, the Programme of Action points to the need for " intensified capital movements and transfers of technical knowledge to promote a reciprocally advantageous international division of labour [which] calls for necessary readjustments in countries of employment ". It thus endorses the objective of substituting trade flows for manpower flows.

The Programme of Action puts forward a set of principles which should govern migration policies and be incorporated in bilateral and multilateral agreements among the sending and receiving countries. It further calls for the setting up of skilled manpower pools or data banks in order to provide reliable information on the availability of job opportunities for workers wishing to emigrate or return to their country of origin.

The ILO is requested to provide various forms of co-operation and technical support in order to assist in the preparation and implementation of such measures as those mentioned above.

On *technologies for productive employment creation*, the Programme of Action urges that " developing countries should arrive at a reasonable balance between labour-intensive and capital-intensive techniques, with a view to achieving the fundamental aim of maximising growth and employment and satisfying basic needs ". Among the proposals for action, it is argued that " it will be helpful to establish national, subregional and regional centres for the transfer and development of technology and to promote co-operation both between developing countries and between the latter and developed countries ". The ILO is requested to help in the establishment of these centres in conjunction with other agencies of the United Nations system.

Developing countries are asked to accelerate appropriate technological advancement in the informal urban and the rural sectors. This is an important point because only too often studies on policy measures concerning the choice of technique concentrate on the modern sector, neglecting the traditional rural and urban informal sectors.

Foreign firms are urged to introduce technologies which are both growth- and employment-generating and to adapt these technologies to the needs of the host countries.

At the international level, better co-ordination of the work being done on appropriate technologies within the United Nations system is needed to ensure that the full potential benefits are realised. The ILO is requested to strengthen its activities in the field of the collection and dissemination of information on appropriate technologies, especially for the rural sector, and to set up a working group on a tripartite basis to examine possible future action on appropriate technology for employment and income distribution and its consequences for vocational training.

Finally, representatives of the Group of 77, the Workers' group and some industrialised countries supported the establishment of a Consultative Group on Appropriate Technology and an International Appropriate Technology Unit, whereas Government and Employers' delegates from most of the Western industrialised countries did not.

On the agenda item concerned with *active manpower policies and adjustment assistance in the developed countries*, the Programme of Action calls upon governments to provide adjustment assistance in order to facilitate the establishment of new economic relations between developing and developed nations, but insists that such assistance should not be at the expense of development aid.

The developed countries are requested, in the implementation of policies to achieve full employment, to continue to pursue and expand trade liberalisation policies in order to increase imports of manufactures and semi-manufactures from developing countries. In this connection, adjustment assistance is considered preferable to import restrictions.

Adjustment assistance should start well before workers lose their jobs, not when unemployment is imminent. This is an important recommendation because it endorses the idea of anticipatory adjustment assistance policies. The Programme of Action goes on to recommend the setting up of regional or national readjustment funds by the industrialised countries or the adaptation of existing funds (for example, the EEC Social and Regional Funds) to assist in the adjustment of industries and workers affected by changes in the international economic situation.

The ILO is requested to contribute to the exchange of information and experience on the functioning and problems of active manpower policies and adjustment assistance. More specifically, the ILO Industrial Committees " could provide a forum for discussing the problems of employment and working conditions resulting from structural change ".

On *the role of multinational enterprises in employment creation in the developing countries*, although a number of valuable suggestions were made by various delegates, it did not prove possible to reach a consensus. Nevertheless, the Programme of Action sets out clearly the views and proposals of the Employers' and Workers' groups, of the Group of 77, and of representatives of the industrialised market-economy and socialist countries. In this connection it is worth noting that, at the request of the ILO Governing Body, the Office is continuing its research into the social consequences of the operations of multinational enterprises.

Conclusion

The World Employment Conference addressed itself to highly complex, controversial and sensitive issues. There are genuine and sharp differences of opinion on these issues among different groups and governments. It was, therefore, a major success that participants were able to reach agreement on the Declaration of Principles and the Programme of Action. It required prolonged and difficult negotiations and a willingness to compromise on the part of all sections of the tripartite constituency of the ILO to achieve this consensus. In the last analysis, the success of the Conference was in large measure due to the universal feeling that the themes before it were too important to risk failure. The Conference was also a proof and reaffirmation of the validity of the principle of tripartism embodied in the ILO.

There was a broad area of concordance between the proposals put forward in the Director-General's report and the final outcome of the Conference. It is true that full consensus could not be achieved in certain areas such as the institutional proposals relating to technological innovation, but there is every expectation that further work in this field will eventually result in agreement. It would not have been realistic to expect agreement on proposals concerned with multinational enterprises. But here again a careful reading of the final document suggests that in a number of areas it should not prove difficult to reach agreement on certain specific proposals in the near future.

In a broader context, the outcome of the World Employment Conference marks a significant advance in the evolution of international thinking on the future social and economic world order. It brings to the centre of world debate and action the basic objectives of economic development—to free mankind from the scourge of poverty, hunger and malnutrition, ill health and illiteracy. The satisfaction of the basic needs of the poor within a generation should provide a simple but powerful unifying theme for national and international development efforts in the years to come.

For the ILO, the outcome of the Conference provides a new and urgent mandate and affords it the opportunity to play a key role in the solution of one of the central problems of our age.

Declaration of principles and Programme of action

adopted by the Tripartite World Conference
on Employment, Income Distribution and Social Progress,
and the International Division of Labour,
Geneva, 4-17 June 1976

DECLARATION OF PRINCIPLES

The Tripartite World Conference on Employment, Income Distribution and Social Progress, and the International Division of Labour held in Geneva from 4 to 17 June 1976 in accordance with the resolution adopted by the International Labour Conference during its 59th Session (1974):

AWARE that past development strategies in most developing countries have not led to the eradication of poverty and unemployment; that the historical features of the development processes in these countries have produced an employment structure characterised by a large proportion of the labour force in rural areas with high levels of underemployment and unemployment; that underemployment and poverty in rural and urban informal sectors and open unemployment, especially in urban areas, has reached such critical dimensions that major shifts in development strategies at both national and international levels are urgently needed in order to ensure full employment and an adequate income to every inhabitant of this one world in the shortest possible time;

AWARE that industrialised countries have not been able to maintain full employment and that economic recession has resulted in widespread unemployment;

NOTING that the Conference is a major initiative on the part of the International Labour Organisation towards the efforts that many of the member countries are making to establish a more equitable international economic order, and that it is consistent with the deliberations of the important world conferences of recent years;

RECALLING further the conclusions of the Sixth and Seventh Special Sessions of the United Nations General Assembly, in particular Resolution 3202 (S-VI) concerning the Establishment of a New International Economic

Order, and Resolution 3362 (S-VII) concerning Development and International Economic Co-operation;

NOTING that underemployment, unemployment, poverty, malnutrition and illiteracy are caused by both national and international factors; that at the national level they are caused by structural factors emanating from under-development and, at the international level, they are due mainly to the deteriorating situation in developing countries, which is partly the consequence of cyclical and structural imbalances in the world economic situation;

RECOGNISING that one of the primary objectives of national development efforts and of international economic relations must be to achieve full employment and to satisfy the basic needs of all people throughout this one world;

COMMITTED to the attainment of an equitable distribution of income and wealth through appropriate strategies to eradicate poverty and promote full, productive employment to satisfy basic needs;

NOTING:

(a) that unemployment, underemployment and marginality are a universal concern and affect at least one-third of humanity at the present time, offending human dignity and preventing the exercise of the right to work;

(b) that the experience of the past two decades has shown that rapid growth of gross national product has not automatically reduced poverty and inequality in many countries, nor has it provided sufficient productive employment within acceptable periods of time;

(c) the current unsatisfactory international economic situation and the discussions of problems affecting unemployment and related issues in UNCTAD IV;

(d) that the existence of an informal urban sector which has grown out of proportion during the past decades in the developing countries and the chronic lack of jobs in rural areas burden the labour markets and hinder the sectoral and regional integration of national development policies;

(e) that it is necessary to replace the current international division of labour wherein the participation of developing countries in international trade is mainly the exportation of raw materials, semi-processed products and highly labour-intensive manufactured goods and the importation of highly capital-intensive industrial products, so as to enable all countries to engage in other types of production in accordance with their national priorities;

RECALLING the Universal Declaration of Human Rights, in particular Article 23, adopted by the General Assembly of the United Nations in 1948;

CONSIDERING that only productive work and gainful employment, without discrimination, enable man to fulfil himself socially and as an individual, and reconfirming that the assured opportunity to work is a basic human right and freedom;

CONSIDERING that the growth of productive employment is one of the most effective means to ensure a just and equitable distribution of income and to raise the standard of living of the majority of the population;

CONVINCED that the establishment and modernisation of small and medium-sized enterprises in rural as well as in urban sectors will increase the volume of employment and therefore play an important part in a basic-needs strategy, and that the private sector has an important role to play in development and employment creation;

CONSIDERING that integrated development of developing countries can be achieved only in so far as equal priority is attached to the social, economic and political aspects of development;

AFFIRMING that the problems of underemployment, unemployment and poverty must be attacked by means of direct, well co-ordinated measures at both national and international levels;

RECOGNISING that in most developing countries, the government is the principal promoter of development and employment and the competent instrument to achieve a just and equitable distribution of income, with the effective participation of trade unions, rural workers' organisations and employers' associations;

RECOGNISING that international relations should be based on co-operation, interdependence, national sovereignty, self-determination of peoples, and non-intervention in the internal affairs of countries;

RECONFIRMING the importance of regional and subregional co-operation as a major instrument to achieve the expansion of domestic markets, to facilitate the use of modern technologies, efficient industrialisation, better integration into the world economy, and to give greater weight to the positions of developing countries in international relations, with a view to accelerating the development of Third World countries;

NOTING the firm commitment of the developing countries and of some developed countries to implement the New International Economic Order, based on the principles contained in the Charter of Economic Rights and Duties of States;

NOTING that a review and appraisal of the strategy for the Second Development Decade (Resolution 3517 of the United Nations General Assembly) are taking place and that preparations for the Third Development Decade have commenced;

CONVINCED that the strategy for the Second Development Decade needs to be complemented by a programme of action to guide international and national development efforts towards fulfilling the basic needs of all the people and particularly the elementary needs of the lowest income groups;

RECALLING that the ILO, particularly through its World Employment Programme, has a direct responsibility for elaborating such a strategy with regard to the achievement of full productive employment in decent working conditions, and ensuring respect for the freedoms and rights of association and collective bargaining laid down in Conventions Nos. 87, 98 and 135;

The Conference hereby adopts this Declaration of Principles and the Programme of Action and requests the Governing Body of the ILO to implement the Programme of Action where appropriate in co-operation with other international organisations.

PROGRAMME OF ACTION

I. BASIC NEEDS

1. Strategies and national development plans and policies should include explicitly as a priority objective the promotion of employment and the satisfaction of the basic needs of each country's population.

2. Basic needs, as understood in this Programme of Action, include two elements. First, they include certain minimum requirements of a family for private consumption: adequate food, shelter and clothing, as well as certain household equipment and furniture. Second, they include essential services provided by and for the community at large, such as safe drinking water, sanitation, public transport and health, educational and cultural facilities.

3. A basic-needs-oriented policy implies the participation of the people in making the decisions which affect them through organisations of their own choice.

4. In all countries freely chosen employment enters into a basic-needs policy both as a means and as an end. Employment yields an output. It provides an income to the employed, and gives the individual a feeling of self-respect, dignity and of being a worthy member of society.

5. It is important to recognise that the concept of basic needs is a country-specific and dynamic concept. The concept of basic needs should be placed within a context of a nation's over-all economic and social development. In no circumstances should it be taken to mean merely the minimum necessary for subsistence; it should be placed within a context of national independence, the dignity of individual and peoples and their freedom to chart their destiny without hindrance.

Strategies and policies to create full employment and to meet basic needs in developing countries

6. In developing countries satisfaction of basic needs cannot be achieved without both acceleration in their economic growth and measures aimed at changing the pattern of growth and access to the use of productive resources by the lowest income groups. Often these measures will require a transformation of social structures, including an initial redistribution of assets, especially land, with adequate and timely compensation. Land reform should be supplemented by rural community development. In some countries, however, public ownership and control of other assets is an essential ingredient of their strategy. Obviously, each country must democratically and independently decide its policies in accordance with its needs and objectives.

7. Any national employment-centred development strategy aiming at satisfying the basic needs of the population as a whole should, however, include the following essential elements, to the extent that countries consider them to be desirable:

Macro-economic policies

(a) An increase in the volume and productivity of work in order to increase the incomes of the lowest income groups;

(b) strengthening the production and distribution system of essential goods and services to correspond with the new pattern of demand;

(c) an increase in resource mobilisation for investment; the introduction of progressive income and wealth taxation policies; the adoption of credit policies to ensure employment creation and increased production of basic goods and services;

(d) the control of the utilisation and processing of natural resources as well as the establishment of basic industries that would generate self-reliant and harmonious economic development;

(e) developing inter-regional trade, especially among the developing countries, in order to promote collective self-reliance and to ensure the satisfaction of basic import needs without depending permanently on external aid;

(f) a planned increase in investments in order to achieve diversification of employment and technological progress and to overcome other regional and sectoral inequalities;

(g) reform of the price mechanism in order to achieve greater equity and efficiency in resource allocation and to ensure sufficient income to small producers;

(h) reform of the fiscal system to provide employment-linked incentives and more socially just patterns of income distribution;

(i) safeguarding ecological and environmental balances;

(j) provision by the government of the policy framework to guide the private and public sectors towards meeting basic needs, and making its own industrial enterprises model employers; in many cases this can only be done in a national planning framework;

(k) the development of human resources through education and vocational training.

Employment policy

8. Member States should place prime emphasis on the generation of employment, in particular to meet the challenge of creating sufficient jobs in developing countries by the year 2000 and thereby achieve full employment. Specific targets should be set to reduce progressively unemployment and under-employment.

9. The following policies should be adopted to encourage employment creation:

(a) Member States should ratify ILO Convention No. 122 and should ratify, implement and safeguard fair labour standards, such as the right to organise and to engage in collective bargaining, as laid down in ILO Conventions Nos. 87, 98 and 135.

(b) In the criteria for project selection and appraisal, employment and income distribution aspects should have adequate emphasis in development planning and in the lending policies of international financial institutions.

(c) Member States should implement active labour market policies of the type set forth in the ILO Human Resources Development Convention, 1975 (No. 142), and the accompanying Human Resources Development Recommendation, 1975 (No. 150), and adjust enterprise-level policies, especially with regard to recruitment, work organisation, working conditions and work content, so as fully to absorb underutilised labour resources.

(d) Wage policies should be such that:

(i)   they ensure minimum levels of living;

(ii) the real wages of workers and the real incomes of self-employed producers are protected and progressively increased;

(iii) wage levels are equitable and reflect relative social productivity;

(iv) anti-inflationary incomes and price policies, where introduced, take these objectives into account.

(e) Equality of treatment and remuneration for women should be ensured.

Rural sector policies

10. Governments should give high priority to rural development, and increase the effectiveness of their policies, including those to reorganise the agrarian structure. Rural development involves the modernisation of agriculture,

the development of agro-based industries, and the provision of both physical and social infrastructure. It should encompass educational and vocational training facilities, the construction of main and feeder roads, the provision of credit facilities and technical assistance, especially to small farmers and agricultural labourers.

11. Co-operatives should be promoted in accordance with ILO Recommendation No. 127 and extend not only to the use of land, equipment and credit, but also to the fields of transportation, storage, marketing and the distribution network, processing and services generally. More emphasis should be placed on the development of co-operatives in national policies, especially when they can be implemented so as to involve the lowest income groups, through their own organisations.

12. In most of the developing countries, agrarian reform, land distribution and the provision of ancillary services are basic to rural development. A minimum requirement is to provide house sites for rural and plantation workers and other landless labourers so as to assist them in building their homes and making them independent, especially in case of loss of employment.

13. The main thrust of a basic-needs strategy must be to ensure that there is effective mass participation of the rural population in the political process in order to safeguard their interests. In view of the highly hierarchical social and economic structure of agrarian societies in some developing countries, measures of redistributive justice are likely to be thwarted unless backed by organisations of rural workers. A policy of active encouragement to small farmers and rural workers' organisations should be pursued to enable them to participate effectively in the implementation of:

(a) programmes of agrarian reforms, distribution of surplus lands and land settlement;

(b) programmes for developing ancillary services such as credit, supply of inputs and marketing; and

(c) programmes concerning other employment generation schemes, such as public works, agro-industries and rural crafts.

As specified in ILO Convention No. 141, governments should create conditions for the development of effective organisations of rural workers.

Social policies

14. Social policies should be designed to increase the welfare of working people, especially women, the young and the aged.

Women

15. Since women constitute the group on the bottom of the ladder in many developing countries in respect of employment, poverty, education,

training and status, the Conference recommends that special emphasis be placed in developing countries on promoting the status, education, development and employment of women and on integrating women into the economic and civic life of the country.

16. Specifically, the Conference recommends:

(a) the abolition of every kind of discrimination as regards the right to work, pay, employment, vocational guidance and training (including in-service training), promotion in employment and access to skilled jobs;

(b) that more favourable working conditions be ensured so that women may perform their other functions in society and married women may be able to return to either full-time or part-time productive employment;

(c) that the work burden and drudgery of women be relieved by improving their working and living conditions and by providing more resources for investment in favour of women in rural areas.

The young, the aged and the handicapped

17. In the implementation of basic-needs strategies, there should be no discrimination against the young, the aged or the handicapped. Every effort should be made to provide the young with productive employment, equal opportunity and equal pay for work of equal value, vocational training and working conditions suited to their age. Exploitation of child labour should be prohibited in accordance with the relevant ILO standards.

Participation of organised groups

18. Governments must try to involve employers' organisations, trade unions and rural workers' and producers' organisations in decision-making procedures and in the process of implementation at all levels. These are the organisations which represent the vast majority of the population and, therefore, they must be the ones to help define the basic needs and apply the necessary strategies.

19. Employers' and producers' organisations, trade unions and other workers' organisations such as rural workers' organisations have an important role to play in the design and implementation of sucessful development strategies. They must be encouraged to participate effectively in the decision-making process. Workers' organisations are also of great importance in the search for a reform of the existing international economic structures and they have a major role to play in the achievement of a fairer distribution of income and wealth.

Education

20. Education is itself a basic need, and equality of access to educational services, particularly in rural areas, is therefore an important ingredient of a

basic-needs strategy. Lack of access to education denies many people, and particularly women, the opportunity to participate fully and meaningfully in the social, economic, cultural and political life of the community.

21. Educational and vocational training systems should be adapted to national development needs and should avoid an élitist bias; priority should be given to adult and primary education, especially in the rural areas.

Population policy

22. High birth rates in poverty-stricken areas are not the cause of under-development but a result of it. They may, however, jeopardise the satisfaction of basic needs. It is only through the fulfilment of these needs, with special emphasis on the development of the position and status of women, that couples will be in a better position to determine the size of their family in a manner compatible with the aims of their society. The Conference is of the view that population policies consistent with the culture and the societies involved, as recommended by the 1974 World Population Conference, should be strongly encouraged. It recommends that information on population programmes should be made available to people in a form and language that they can understand.

International economic co-operation

23. The satisfaction of basic needs is a national endeavour, but its success depends crucially upon strengthening world peace and disarmament and the establishment of a New International Economic Order. The World Employment Conference fully supports the efforts being made by the United Nations General Assembly in its resolution as adopted at the Seventh Special Session and through the relevant agencies of the UN system to introduce international reforms in trade and finance in favour of developing countries and thus to contribute to the creation of a New International Economic Order. The Conference recognises that the basic-needs strategy is only the first phase of the redistributive global growth process.

24. In particular, the Conference, recognising the primary objectives of national development, urges ILO member States to continue their efforts through the appropriate UN agencies to:

(a) stabilise developing countries' exports of primary products and improve their terms of trade through financing an integrated commodity programme;

(b) secure expanded access for developing countries' manufactured exports to the markets of rich countries through trade liberalisation measures on a non-reciprocal basis;

(c) increase the net transfer of resources to developing countries, including the mitigation of their debt burden;

(d) increase mutual economic co-operation between countries with different social and economic systems.

25. The Employers' group wished it to be placed on record that they regarded the section on international economic co-operation as being outside the proper competence of the ILO and as being inappropriate for comment by employers. They agreed, however, that the ILO should co-operate with relevant UN organisations, wherever appropriate, in implementing its policies throughout the developing world.

26. A number of Western industrialised countries wished it to be placed on record that they regarded the section on international economic co-operation (paras. 23 and 24) as being outside the proper competence of the ILO. They took the view that, within its area of competence, the ILO should co-operate with other UN organisations, wherever appropriate, in implementing its policies throughout the developing world.

Recommendations

27. The ILO should co-operate with other UN agencies in bringing about these desired reforms in order to give meaning and reality to the expressed commitment of the world community to assist national basic-needs strategies. It should work through, in particular, the World Employment Programme, including its regional components, and its recognised instrumentalities, such as the existing standard-setting activities, technical assistance and industrial activities.

28. The ILO should, in particular, undertake promotion of short-term and quick employment-generating programmes for making an immediate impact on the prevailing levels of poverty and massive waste of human resources. The Conference recommends that a portion of the $1,000 million International Fund for Agricultural Development should be used for the generation of employment in the rural sector.

29. The Governing Body of the ILO is urged to recommend the review of research programmes, operational activities and organisational structures of the UN family so as to focus them more sharply on the contribution they can make to meeting the basic-needs targets, particularly of the lowest income groups. The Administrative Committee on Co-ordination (ACC) should be requested to review, monitor and report on the work of the different agencies and regional commissions of the UN system.

30. The ILO should, in co-operation both with other UN bodies and with interested national governments, consider the feasibility of initiating a world-wide programme in support of household surveys to map the nature, extent and causes of poverty; to assist countries to set up the necessary statistical and monitoring services; and to measure progress toward the fulfilment of basic needs.

31. Member States should, to the extent possible, supply the ILO, before the end of the decade, with the following information:

(a) a quantitative evaluation of basic needs for the lowest income groups within their population, preferably based on the findings of a tripartite commission established for the purpose;

(b) a description of policies, existing and in preparation, in order to implement the basic-needs strategy.

32. The ILO is requested to prepare a report for an annual conference before the end of the decade and to include the following information:

(a) an elaboration of more precise concepts defining basic needs on the basis of national replies;

(b) a survey of the entire range of national replies received and an analysis of the national situations with respect to the levels of basic needs as well as policies to attain them.

33. The Governing Body of the ILO is urged to place the question of the revision of Convention No. 122 on the agenda of an early session of the International Labour Conference.

Planned migration for employment: would-be migrants being screened for employment under a bilateral agreement

34. The Conference finally requests that policies required to meet basic needs become an essential part of the United Nations Second Development Decade Strategy and form the core of the Third Development Decade Strategy.

II. INTERNATIONAL MANPOWER MOVEMENTS AND EMPLOYMENT

General objectives of national and international policies

35. The aim of national and international policies in this field should be threefold: (i) to provide more attractive alternatives to migration in the country of origin; (ii) to protect migrants and their families from the difficulties and distress which sometimes follow migration; (iii) to take care that neither migration nor its alternatives are prejudicial to the rest of the population or harmful to economic and social development in either the country of origin or the country of employment.

Measures designed to avoid the need for workers to emigrate

36. The development strategy in the countries of origin should include in particular an employment policy which would give workers productive employment and satisfactory conditions of work and life.

37. This strategy should be implemented in the framework of multilateral and bilateral co-operation which would make it possible through such means as encouragement of appropriate intensified capital movements and transfers of technical knowledge to promote a reciprocally advantageous international division of labour; this calls for necessary readjustments in countries of employment.

Measures against migrations in abusive conditions and in favour of the promotion of equality of opportunity and treatment

38. Governments, employers and workers of the countries of employment should ensure that all migrants are protected against any exploitation and effectively enjoy equality of opportunity and treatment. These principles and the means of implementing them are stated in detail in the international standards of the ILO and more specifically in the Migrant Workers (Supplementary Provisions) Convention, 1975 (No. 143), and in the complementary Migrant Workers Recommendation, 1975 (No. 151). A special effort should be made to ratify and apply the Convention and give effect to the provisions of the Recommendation, especially with regard to:

(a) the fight against migrations in abusive conditions, particularly through sanctions in conformity with Article 6 of the Convention;

(b) the promotion of equality of opportunity and treatment in respect of employment and occupation, of social security, of trade union and cultural

rights and of individual and collective freedoms and especially the encouragement of the efforts of migrant workers and their families to preserve their national and ethnic identity as well as their cultural ties with their country of origin, including the possibility for children to be given some knowledge of their mother tongue;

(c) the elaboration and implementation of a social policy which emphasises:

(i)   reunification of families;
(ii) protection of the health of migrant workers;
(iii) establishment of adequate social services;

(d) minimum guarantees as regards employment and residence.

39. In order to combat discrimination and illegal trafficking in manpower, governments, employers and workers should strengthen their action to ensure the application of national legislation and collective agreements and to initiate the early introduction of appropriate penal sanctions against all who organise or knowingly take advantage of illegal movements of manpower.

Multilateral and bilateral agreements

40. Multilateral and bilateral agreements should be drawn up to deal with the migration of workers and problems concerning migrant workers and their families. Such agreements should be in accordance with the principles established in ILO standards. As far as possible, representative organisations of employers and workers should participate in their preparation and implementation.

41. Such agreements should be based upon the economic and social needs of the countries of origin and the countries of employment; they should take account not only of short-term manpower needs and resources, but also of the long-term social and economic consequences of migration, for migrants as well as for the communities concerned.

42. One of the principal objectives of mutually accepted policies in the framework of these agreements should be to even out fluctuations in migration movements, return migration flows and remittances and make them as far as possible predictable, continuous and assured so as to facilitate the implementation of long-term programmes of economic and social development.

43. Taking into account the economic and social circumstances in the countries and regions concerned and the characteristics of the migration movements concerned, these agreements should in appropriate cases:

(a) facilitate the co-ordination of employment policies, especially in the framework of efforts for economic and social integration on a regional basis;

(b) regulate the recruitment of migrant workers without discrimination and according to their free choice under the auspices of the employment services of the countries concerned;

(c) provide for periodic exchange of information between the countries concerned on the occupational categories and the number of workers to whom contracts could be offered and who would be ready to emigrate or return to their country of origin; for this purpose skilled manpower pools or data banks should be established to provide reliable information on the supply of and demand for skilled, professional and technical manpower;

(d) reinforce co-operation between the employment and other services dealing with migration and migrant workers in the countries concerned;

(e) give priority to the recruitment of workers who are underemployed or unemployed;

(f) provide that countries of origin should adopt appropriate measures so as to avoid the departure of skilled workers, including adaptation of education and training schemes to national needs and offering highly trained personnel conditions permitting them to remain and serve their own country;

(g) provide that countries of employment should refrain from recruiting skilled and highly skilled workers when there are recognised or potential shortages of such workers in the country of origin;

(h) provide that the countries of employment could take complementary measures to aid the developing countries to minimise their loss of qualified manpower, for example by increasing training possibilities for their own nationals in those fields where skills are scarce and by eliminating any part of their immigration laws and regulations which have the effect of encouraging the entry of professional and other highly qualified migrants;

(i) provide ways of limiting losses in countries of origin, particularly developing countries, which may result from the departure of skilled personnel whose education and training they have provided;

(j) establish training facilities, where these do not already exist, making possible:

(i) suitable preparation, documentation and training of candidates for emigration;

(ii) vocational training and advancement of migrant workers in the country of employment;

(iii) training of workers wishing to return to the countries of origin, taking account of the aptitudes of such workers and the needs of their countries;

(k) adopt the necessary measures to facilitate the voluntary return to their countries of origin of migrant workers and their resettlement;

(l) provide for social security benefits for families which have stayed in the country of origin and for suitable means of ensuring that migrant workers returning to their home countries enjoy continuity of social security benefits;

(m) take into consideration the need for financing the above measures by appropriate means.

The role of the ILO

44. At their request, the ILO should provide technical co-operation to the countries concerned and technical support to regional organisations in order to make it possible to prepare and implement the above measures.

45. At the request of governments concerned, the ILO should study the possibility of setting up at regional or subregional level a system designed with the collaboration of the representative employers' and workers' organisations concerned to improve information on the availability of job opportunities in certain industries and certain types of employment for the benefit of candidates for emigration or return to their country of origin.

46. The Office should:

(a) initiate studies on the economic and social effects of different kinds of migration for employment;

(b) make studies and organise meetings at regional or subregional levels on the problems of migrant workers who have not been regularly admitted or who lack official papers.

The development of human resources through education and training

III. TECHNOLOGIES FOR PRODUCTIVE EMPLOYMENT CREATION IN DEVELOPING COUNTRIES

Policy objectives

47. Technology has an important role to play in the process of development. Since technology is linked with the choice of products as well as with capital investment, labour and skills required to produce them, it has a bearing on the level of productive employment and the distribution of income. Technology, therefore, is an important element of the basic-needs strategy, which must be part of an over-all national, economic and social development strategy.

48. There is an urgent need for appropriate and optimal technology, that is, management and production techniques which are best suited to the resources and future development potential of developing countries. Such technology should contribute to greater productive employment opportunities, elimination of poverty and the achievement of equitable income distribution.

49. The exclusive use of labour-intensive techniques will neither solve the problems of the developing countries nor reduce their dependence on industrialised countries. Likewise, the exclusive use of capital-intensive techniques will present the developing countries with serious problems: financial difficulties, lack of managerial staff and supervisory personnel and delays in the solution to employment problems. Thus developing countries should arrive at a reasonable balance between labour-intensive and capital-intensive techniques, with a view to achieving the fundamental aim of maximising growth and employment and satisfying basic needs. This strategy of equilibrium between the various types of technologies should also take account of the desire to adopt advanced techniques, with a view to reducing the existing technological gap between countries.

50. Choice, development and transfer of technology require that proper emphasis should be placed on the building up of national infrastructure for human resources development, particularly to promote training of workers, technicians and managers for appropriate technology selection.

51. In the selection of new technologies appropriate to their needs, the developing countries should take due account of the need to protect their ecology and natural resources. There is also a need to pay due attention to social aspects, working conditions and the safety of workers when introducing new technologies.

Action at the national level

52. The choice of appropriate technologies is dependent on the conditions prevailing in each country and the characteristics of each economic sector. This choice must also be based on the full utilisation of national resources. Thus each developing country has the right and duty to choose the technologies

which it decides are appropriate. To facilitate such a choice, it will be helpful to establish national subregional and regional centres for the transfer and development of technology and to promote co-operation both between developing countries and between the latter and developed countries. The ILO should help in the establishment of these centres in conjunction with other agencies of the UN system.

53. The promotion of research should be a fundamental priority in policies to increase the national technological capacity of developing countries and reduce their dependence on industrialised countries. This research should mainly be undertaken within, and under the direction of, the developing countries themselves or in corresponding regional or subregional bodies where these exist, with the technical and financial assistance of international and other agencies presently involved in such activities. Technological research should furthermore contribute towards the satisfaction of basic needs.

54. Each developing country should accelerate appropriate technological advancement in the informal urban and rural sectors, in particular, to eliminate underemployment and unemployment and raise productivity levels.

55. Foreign firms, in response to the national legislation of developing countries and in negotiation with them, and taking into account the national economic development plans, should:

(a) introduce technologies which are both growth- and employment-generating, directly or indirectly;

(b) adapt technologies to the needs of the host countries, and progressively substitute national for imported technology;

(c) contribute to financing the training of national managers and technicians for the better utilisation and generation of technology;

(d) supply resources and direct technical assistance for national and regional technology research; and

(e) spread technological knowledge and help in its growth by subcontracting the production of parts and materials to national producers, and particularly to small producers.

56. Each developing country should accelerate the formulation and implementation of a training plan at the following levels:

(a) middle-level technicians and skilled workers to be employed in the production technologies associated with the goods and services required to satisfy basic needs;

(b) professionals, technicians, managers and skilled workers to replace expatriate staff who presently apply advanced technology;

(c) professionals and technicians needed to manage research and studies undertaken by national and/or regional technological research bodies; and

(d) technicians, professionals and skilled workers, who should be assured of a measure of social status and incentives to prevent a brain drain, in order to promote the utilisation of technologies designed to achieve material and social objectives.

Action at the international level

57. International agencies and bilateral and multi-bilateral aid programmes should devote resources and technical assistance to complement developing countries' efforts.

58. At present several organisations of the UN system are engaged in work on appropriate technologies for developing countries. Better co-ordination of this work would ensure that the full potential benefits may be realised.

59. The UN Interagency Task Force on Information Exchange and the Transfer of Technology is working towards the establishment of a network for the exchange of technological information. At its second session in May 1976 it recommended that:

> organisations of the United Nations system and other organisations having substantive responsibility in the field of technological information and the transfer of technology should develop their relevant activities as components of the over-all network, and in mutual co-operation make available their own information bases and information-handling capabilities as appropriate.

The ILO should strengthen its activities in the field of the collection and dissemination of information on appropriate technologies, especially for the rural sector, and so make an important contribution towards the establishment of the information exchange network referred to above.

60. The ILO should reorient and strengthen its existing programme in order to provide more manpower training and human resources development in the developing countries.

61. The ILO should pursue its research and technical co-operation in the field of development and transfer of technology. It should set up a Working Group in which employers and workers would be represented to examine action on appropriate technology for employment, vocational training and income distribution. The developing countries should participate directly in this Working Group, which should not encroach upon the activities of other UN agencies.

62. The Group of 77 endorsed the establishment of a Consultative Group on Appropriate Technology and an International Appropriate Technology Unit, especially directed to research on the choice of alternative use of resources allowing a greater utilisation of labour per unit of investment, provided that such mechanisms are integrated with the ongoing activities of

A significant proportion of mankind continues to eke out an existence in the most abject conditions of material deprivation ▷

the UN system. The Workers' group also endorsed these proposals but emphasised that these bodies should be tripartite in character. Most Western industrialised countries did not support these two proposals. The Workers' group and the Group of 77 supported the UNCTAD proposal for an international code of conduct for technology transfer. This should be of a legally binding, not voluntary, nature. They further supported the suggestion that the Paris Convention of 1883 on industrial property should be drastically revised.

IV. ACTIVE MANPOWER POLICIES AND ADJUSTMENT ASSISTANCE IN DEVELOPED COUNTRIES

General principles

63. Governments of developed countries should pursue a determined policy to achieve and maintain full employment, i.e. to provide employment opportunities for all those who want to work, and contribute to a fair distribution of income and wealth in these countries. Employment policy should be closely integrated with over-all economic policy and national planning. It has to be related to other social policies.

64. The success of active manpower policies pursued with this aim will facilitate adaptation to structural changes including those which result from

expanding trade with developing countries, thereby supporting growth and increased employment in these countries. Employment policy should not exclusively be based on measures to influence general demand. It should also be based on a range of selective measures to create new job opportunities. Such selective measures should also make a contribution to the struggle against inflation. Governments in the industrialised countries should strengthen the co-ordination of economic policies to maintain full employment. Measures should also be taken to ensure close collaboration concerning the migratory movement of workers between countries of origin and reception.

65. This policy will contribute to a high level of economic activity and improvements in the international economic order as called for by the UN General Assembly, and will lead to increased trade with the developing countries, thus increasing growth and employment in these countries.

66. Structural changes resulting from modifications in the international economic order must not take place at the expense of workers. Such changes should contribute to job creation in both industrialised and developing countries, and assure suitable employment to all workers, involving countries of whatever social and political system. The governments concerned should provide adjustment assistance in order to facilitate the establishment of new economic relations between developing and developed nations. It is envisaged that such adjustment assistance would not diminish development aid.

Policy measures

67. The priorities of national employment policies should be:

(i) the maintenance of as high a demand for labour as is necessary in order to achieve full employment;

(ii) measures and policies to promote stable economic growth, which should include both general and selective measures;

(iii) the reinforcement of measures designed to provide protection against undesirable effects of cyclical evolution or structural change, such as those mentioned in ILO Conventions and Recommendations.

These measures could include:

– provision of maximum practicable notice of change for workers whose jobs are threatened;

– provision of appropriate income levels for a reasonable period and the safeguarding of pension rights;

– provision of retraining;

– provision of special measures for women, migrants, young workers, and handicapped workers whose re-employment involves special problems.

These matters should be dealt with in close co-operation between governments, employers and workers.

68. Many of these features already exist in the policies of industrialised countries.

69. In implementing employment and manpower policies, the industrialised countries should continue to pursue and expand trade liberalisation policies in order to increase imports of manufactures and semi-manufactures from developing countries in an effort to increase their employment and incomes, while continuing to maintain employment in industrialised countries. Adjustment assistance is considered preferable to import restrictions.

70. Consistent with national laws and systems, adjustment assistance should start well before workers lose their jobs, when this can be clearly established, and not only when unemployment is imminent.

71. Regional or national readjustment funds could be set up by the industrialised countries or existing funds (for example the EEC Social and Regional Funds) could be adapted for the purpose of assisting in the adjustment of industries and workers affected by changes in the international economic situation. This ought not to reduce development aid.

72. The competitiveness of new imports from developing countries should not be achieved to the detriment of fair labour standards.

73. The World Employment Conference expresses the hope that the discussions in the Multilateral Trade Negotiations concerning the GATT safeguard clause, i.e. GATT Article 19, will lead to improvements in the international safeguard system.

74. Governments and employers' and workers' organisations shall work together to improve industrial life. Employers and workers should consider participation by workers in matters of recognised mutual concern.

Proposals for an ILO action programme

75. The traditional role of the ILO regarding labour standards should be continued in order to ensure respect for fair labour standards in developing and industrialised countries alike.

76. The ILO could contribute to the exchange of information and experience on the functioning and problems of active manpower policies and adjustment assistance. The Workers' members felt that the ILO could, within its special competence and in the context of multilateral trade negotiations, contribute to the improvement of an international safeguard system covering employment and income guarantees, fair labour standards and adjustment measures.

77. ILO Industrial Committees could provide a forum for discussing the problems of employment and working conditions resulting from structural change.

The work-burden and drudgery of women ▷

78. The Turin Centre, CINTERFOR and other regional vocational training centres have an essential role to play in training, a role which could usefully be widened into areas not currently covered.

V. THE ROLE OF MULTINATIONAL ENTERPRISES IN EMPLOYMENT CREATION IN THE DEVELOPING COUNTRIES

The Conference was unable to reach a consensus on the role of multinational enterprises in developing countries. The following paragraphs reflect the position of the different parties.

Declarations of Government members

79. Some governments stressed the positive aspects of the activities of multinational enterprises in developing countries, which they saw as direct employment creation, the linkage effects on the economy, the firms' contribution to an improvement of training, the creation of social services, etc.

80. Some governments stressed that multinational corporations had a role to play in the implementation of a basic-needs strategy. However, it is necessary first to identify the different types of corporation according to their objectives in order to determine which ones could be expected to contribute to the implementation of a basic-needs strategy.

81. Some governments on the other hand underlined the negative effects of the activities of multinational corporations in developing countries, which they saw as the creation of an international division of labour unfavourable to these countries, the control of raw materials, the lack of respect for the sovereign rights of States, the insecurity of the employment provided, the lack of respect for trade union rights and notably the expatriation of profits.

82. Some governments felt that efforts should be made to try to reinforce co-operation between host countries and multinational enterprises, especially through the creation of a favourable climate for private foreign investments. In addition, according to these governments, multinational corporations should not be treated less favourably than local companies.

83. Other governments expressed the opinion that the application of discriminatory measures with regard to multinational enterprises as opposed to local enterprises was one of the sovereign rights of States.

84. The Government members of countries belonging to the Group of 77 based their position on Resolution 3201 adopted by the General Assembly of the United Nations on 1 April 1974 on the establishment of a New International Economic Order based on equity, equality, sovereign rights, interdependence, common interests and co-operation between all States regardless

of their economic and social systems, as well as on the conclusions and recommendations adopted by the Fourth Conference of Non-Aligned Countries in Algiers. These countries stated that transnational enterprises were responsible for the world-wide economic imbalance, that they infringed the sovereignty of States, and that they sometimes tended to constitute monopolies and to engage in market sharing and fixing prices. These governments maintained that all action vis-à-vis transnational enterprises must be taken within the framework of a global strategy conceived to bring about quantitative and qualitative changes in the present system of economic and financial relations. They recalled the sovereign rights of States and condemned all interference in the internal matters of the countries in which transnational enterprises invested.

85. The member countries of the Group of 77 recommended strengthening national enterprises to enable them to take necessary steps with a view to preventing the negative effects of the activities of transnational corporations (TNCs). They also recommended that member States and the ILO continue to provide full support to the activities of the UN Commission on Transnational Corporations to regulate the activities of such enterprises particularly in relation to the Code of Conduct which TNCs should observe, containing the following basic principles:

(i)   TNCs must be subject to the laws and regulations of the host country and in the event of a dispute accept the exclusive jurisdiction of the courts of the country in which they operate;

(ii)   TNCs should refrain from all interference in the internal affairs of the States in which they operate;

(iii)   TNCs should refrain from interference in their relations between the government of the host country and other States, and from influencing these relations;

(iv)   TNCs should not serve as an instrument of the external policy of another State nor as a means of extending to the host country juridical regulations of the country of origin;

(v)   TNCs should be subject to the permanent sovereignty which the host country exercises over all its wealth, natural resources and economic activities;

(vi)   TNCs should comply with national development policies, objectives and priorities and make a contribution to their implementation;

(vii)   TNCs should supply the government of the host country with relevant information on their activities in order to ensure that those activities are in accordance with the national development policies, objectives and priorities of the host country;

(viii) TNCs should conduct their operations in such a way that they result in a net inflow of financial resources for the host country;

(ix)   TNCs should contribute to the development of the domestic, scientific and technological capacity of the host countries;

(x) TNCs should refrain from restrictive trade practices;

(xi) TNCs should respect the socio-cultural identity of the host country.

86. The Group of 77 also recommended that developing countries adopt measures at the national, regional and international levels in order to ensure that transnational enterprises should reorient their activities so as to undertake further manufacturing processes in developing countries and processing in those countries of raw materials for national or foreign markets. They also recommended that the ILO and member States co-operate with a view to bringing the UN Commission on Transnational Corporations to consider among the points to be included in the compulsory Code of Conduct of TNCs those concerning the obligation of these enterprises to hire local labour, not to discriminate against local workers in respect of salaries, conditions of work, training, promotion and access to different levels of seniority. And lastly they recommended that developing countries take steps in order to regulate and control the activities of transnational enterprises so as to ensure that they would act as a positive factor supporting the efforts of developing countries to expand their exports, through the direct impact which the diversification and expansion of such exports can have on the generation of productive employment.

87. The Group of 77 considered that, in conformity with the policies laid down in national development plans, and adhering to the national laws and priorities, and fully respecting the sovereignty of the host countries, the transnational corporations should:

(i) introduce technologies which are both growth- and employment-generating, directly or indirectly;

(ii) adapt technologies to the needs of the host countries;

(iii) contribute to financing the training of national managers and technicians for the better utilisation of technology;

(iv) supply resources and direct technical assistance for national and regional technology research;

(v) spread technological knowledge and help in its growth by sub-contracting the production of parts and materials to national producers and particularly to small producers;

(vi) disclose and fully make available to the host countries all the technical know-how and information involved in production maintenance, design construction, research and development, etc.

88. The Group of 77 supported the proposals of the Workers' group set out in paragraph 118 (i)—(v) below, in particular the suggestion that the ILO Governing Body should place the issue of transnational enterprises and social policy on the agenda of the 1978 Session of the International Labour Conference in order that Conventions on TNCs should be adopted in the

following areas: industrial relations, employment and training, conditions of life and work.

89. Government members of the European socialist countries supported in principle the position of the Group of 77 as well as that of the Workers' members, and endorsed the proposal to place the issue of multinational enterprises and social policy on the agenda of the International Labour Conference in 1978. They felt that in the countries where multinational enterprises operated, they should contribute to employment creation without hindering either a just distribution of incomes or social progress. They underlined that States had an unconditional right to control the activities of multinational enterprises, and that these enterprises must respect the sovereign rights of States and must not interfere in their internal affairs.

90. Most Government members of industrialised market economy countries underlined the positive effects of the activities of multinational enterprises on the economic development of developing countries. These governments underlined the importance of the task of all countries concerned in assisting the economic development of the Third World. They were of the opinion that the multinational enterprises could contribute to the economic development of the host country, especially through the creation of employment. The governments of home countries of multinational enterprises, while considering their own national requirements, should continue to apply selective incentives for foreign investments in such a way as to encourage investments which met the basic needs of the host country. Countries which welcomed foreign investment should create a favourable and stable investment climate which encouraged multinational enterprises to adapt their activities to the economic needs of the country. For this purpose the governments of the host countries should avoid introducing or maintaining inequalities of treatment between multinational enterprises and domestic enterprises in social matters affecting their respective workers.

91. Most Government members of industrialised market economy countries expressed the hope that such policies would help in taking full advantage of the positive aspects of the activities of multinational enterprises. In this spirit these Government members noted the recommendations of the ILO Tripartite Advisory Meeting on the Relationship of Multinational Enterprises and Social Policy, held in Geneva from 4 to 13 May 1976, that appropriate arrangements be made with a view to preparing an ILO Tripartite Declaration of Principles concerning Multinational Enterprises and Social Policy, which would provide the ILO's input into the much broader Code of Conduct which is currently considered by the United Nations Commission on Transnational Corporations. The interests of both the host countries and multinational enterprises were best served, in the long run, by an atmosphere of mutual trust, in which the rules for inter-relationship were known in advance and strictly observed, relevant information was available to all parties concerned, and negotiations were conducted in a flexible manner.

92. In the light of the above, the Government members of industrialised market economy countries were of the opinion that the present contributions of multinational enterprises to the creation of employment in the developing countries could be further increased through various measures such as:

(i) local subcontracting when this was technically possible;

(ii) a progressive increase in the local processing of raw materials;

(iii) local reinvestment of profits to the greatest extent possible;

(iv) replacement of expatriates and maximum utilisation of local personnel;

(v) training and promotion of local production workers and of local management personnel;

(vi) co-operation on matters of training between the multinational enterprises and the various local institutions providing training.

It should be understood, however, that the role the multinational enterprise could play in employment creation varied from one host country to another, from one time-period to another, and from one firm to another. On the other hand, the contribution of multinational corporations could only be partial since the reduction of unemployment in developing countries was a global task, the responsibility for which lay primarily with governments. It was therefore up to them to ensure that the contribution of multinational corporations to employment creation was maximised. The multinational enterprises should respect the sovereign rights of States as well as the relevant laws, rules and national practices and recognised international obligations, it being understood that it would be desirable to refer to Conventions and Recommendations of the ILO when legal, political and economic considerations so permitted. Multinational enterprises should adapt the activities of their subsidiaries to the development programmes and economic objectives of the countries where they were established. This adaptation should take into account all the economic and social factors of these countries.

93. Government members of the industrialised market economy countries considered that it was necessary to reinforce the technical negotiating capacity of developing countries vis-à-vis the multinational corporations. For this purpose:

(i) it recommended that the ILO should study regulations in the employment and training fields, adopted by developing countries, regarding foreign investment and multinational corporations;

(ii) it would be desirable to clarify the need for training in developing countries for the purpose of dealing with foreign investment and to establish corresponding training programmes which would assist governments in negotiating with multinationals on matters relating directly or indirectly to employment creation and the improvement of training;

(iii) it was desirable that the ILO, to the extent of its competence, should be ready to provide technical assistance as required in those fields to governments which requested it.

Also it would be desirable to ask the ILO to carry out studies on employment, training and wages policies adopted by developing countries regarding multinational enterprises. Research should equally be strengthened in the field of appropriate technology and labour-intensive goods, the production of which should be promoted in developing countries.

94. Certain Government members of developing countries associated themselves with most of the proposals in paragraphs 92 and 93 above.

95. Government members of industrialised market economy countries felt that multinational enterprises should so far as possible devote themselves to stepping up research and development in the field of appropriate technology and to the development of products to further employment creation. And that, lastly, for their part, governments should be able, before accepting the investment of multinationals on their territory, to be sure that the techniques proposed were those most suited to employment creation, taking account also of other factors affecting production and marketing.

96. Certain representatives of industrialised market economies, whilst in agreement with certain general points made in paragraphs 90 to 93 above, nevertheless expressed their sympathy vis-à-vis the declaration of the Group of 77. They also expressed their agreement with the procedures proposed in the Tripartite Advisory Meeting of May 1976, as well as with the proposal for research which the ILO could undertake in collaboration with the United Nations Commission on Transnational Corporations, without this implying, however, an acceptance of all the conclusions of that meeting. In addition they stated that it was necessary to co-ordinate the ILO's activities on multinational enterprises with those of the UN Commission on Transnational Corporations.

97. Certain governments, while recognising the importance of a Code of Conduct regulating the activities of multinational enterprises, put the stress on relations of a bilateral character which can exist between host countries and multinational enterprises and on the importance of national regulations for controlling the activities of these enterprises.

Declarations of the Employers' members

98. The Employers' members stated clearly that the relevant agenda item, as determined by the Governing Body at its 196th (May 1975) Session, called for a discussion of "the role of multinational enterprises in employment creation in the developing countries" and that they were prepared to discuss this specific question. They considered that companies in general, including multinational enterprises, as well as governments and trade unions, had a responsibility to bring about a better balance in the distribution of the world's products and knowledge. Multinational enterprises in conjunction with home and host governments and trade unions had an important role to play in advanc-

ing social progress. It was not possible for multinational enterprises to solve the problem of employment and to meet the basic needs of the world, but they had a contribution to make in this field; nevertheless, the responsibility of this task lay primarily with governments.

99. The Employers' members stressed that the discussion of the problem should concentrate on which kind of employment opportunities multinational enterprises could create. These enterprises did concern themselves with developing new activities important for employment, for example in agriculture. Although direct creation of employment by multinational enterprises was limited, the indirect effects were significant and could stimulate national economic development and know-how.

100. They believed that it was up to each government to decide what kinds of industrial activities and technologies were best suited to meet the development needs of its country. New activities of multinational enterprises in developing countries should fit into national plans. Agriculture should be given priority attention in developing countries, and multinational enterprises could provide assistance in developing the production of industrial inputs to agriculture and in building up industries processing agricultural outputs.

101. The Employers' members stressed that multinational enterprises were a significant vehicle for the transfer of advanced technology, that choice of technology was often dictated by governments and that governments of developing countries generally insisted upon the most sophisticated kinds of technology.

102. They further expressed the view that multinational enterprises had beneficial effects on wages and working conditions. It was for host governments to define the social obligations under which multinational enterprises should function. It was the general practice of multinational enterprises to recognise workers' rights as well as the maintenance of labour standards and working conditions. In general, multinationals were responsible, did train local staff, had good industrial relations, had pay scales as good as, or better than, those of national companies, and worked within national regulations. Multinational enterprises were entitled to a fair remuneration for their efforts.

103. The Employer's members pointed out that multinational enterprises were free not to invest and that foreign investors needed a stable investment climate. Tough rules were acceptable as long as they were not arbitrarily changed. Moreover, multinational enterprises objected to regulations which were not applicable also to national companies. The Employers' members insisted on equal treatment on social matters.

104. Taking cognisance of the five reports prepared by the ILO at the request of the Tripartite Meeting on the Relationship between the Multinational Corporations and Social Policy which met in Geneva from 26 October to

4 November 1972 and of the agreed conclusions reached at the Tripartite Advisory Meeting on the Relationships of Multinational Enterprises and Social Policy of 4-12 May 1976, the Employers' members believed that it was not the mission of the World Employment Conference to discuss the content of principles to govern multinational enterprises. A voluntary code of conduct could be helpful.

105. The Employers' members considered that the ILO study on international principles and guidelines was a clear and comprehensive survey of possibilities in the ILO context. The ILO studies had shown that the multinational in general behaved responsibly. They had failed to reveal the existence of problems of the kind referred to by the Workers' members. The multinationals had been shown in the ILO studies to be a force for economic development. Indeed, they were the most effective means yet found for reducing the time-span for producing the management skills needed to organise resources and muster finance. It was necessary to be careful that any action taken would not have adverse implications for the future. The Employers' members were therefore unconvinced of the need for international action in regard to multinationals in the social field. In particular, they considered that any move towards the adoption of an international labour Convention in this area risked creating an impossible situation through the variations in the extent of ratification or acceptance in different countries—a risk mentioned in the ILO study. There was also a question of discriminatory treatment. The bulk of the existing Conventions were of general application, the exceptions to this being so narrow in scope that there was no analogy between them and the wide range of enterprises and industries covered by the term "multinational", with their varying degrees of foreign and national ownership. A Convention applying to all employees of any enterprise under any degree of foreign ownership would place these employees under special regulations that might well be more favourable than those in the prevailing industrial economy of the country, with adverse effects on the orderly conduct of industrial relations. Having regard to the variety of industrial relations patterns and behaviour in different countries, the Employers' members believed that such matters must primarily be determined by the governments of the country concerned and the ordinary law and practice of the country.

106. Another approach that had been suggested was the preparation of a tripartite declaration of principles which could eventually be embodied in more comprehensive United Nations guidelines. The Office study had pointed to the guidance given in Conference resolutions and conclusions of Industrial Committees and other advisory meetings as indicating the feasibility of such a procedure. The Employers' members were not against guidelines in principle, as shown by those published by the International Chamber of Commerce as long ago as 1972 and the active participation of their organisation in OECD's work on a code. The Employers' members were, however, convinced that such

a declaration would not be useful and might well be harmful unless the guidelines met the following points:

(a) that they ensure that the operations of multinational enterprises can continue effectively to the benefit of society as a whole;

(b) that they are non-mandatory but mutually agreed through a tripartite declaration of principles on responsible behaviour for multinational enterprises, governments and trade unions;

(c) that they ensure in social matters that all parties respect the laws and regulations of the host country;

(d) that they recognise the principle of equal treatment for foreign-owned and for national enterprises in matters of industrial relations and social policy;

(e) that they do not bind multinationals to observance of ILO standards not ratified or accepted by the host country, or introduce a system of standards making existing ILO Conventions and Recommendations applicable only to multinational enterprises;

(f) that they are flexible enough to permit application to very different national situations and national objectives and in regard to widely different types of companies and industries;

(g) that they apply effectively to enterprises with public or mixed ownership as well as to privately owned companies.

Restrictive legislation would only slow down employment creation in developing countries by multinational enterprises. Multinational enterprises were already subject to many regulations and governments had adequate powers of their own, any of which could frustrate a company's expectations of a reasonable return.

107. The Employers' members stated that, following the proposal in paragraph 106 above, the Tripartite Advisory Meeting had recommended that a small tripartite group should be established to draft a voluntary declaration of principles applying to multinational enterprises, governments and trade unions. In view of this, the Employers' members did not consider it appropriate to place the question of multinational enterprises and social policy on the agenda of the International Labour Conference in 1978.

108. The Employers' members, after two weeks of discussion, were reluctantly forced to accept that no consensus existed in the group because the differing views of Government, Workers' and Employers' members were irreconcilable.

109. The representatives of employers of European socialist countries fully supported the point of view of the Government members of the European socialist countries with regard to the role of multinational enterprises in employment creation in developing countries.

Declarations of the Workers' members

110. The Workers' members expressed the concerns and preoccupations of trade unions and workers with regard to the effects of the activities of multinational enterprises on employment and more generally on development. They declared that the questions raised under item 4 in Chapter 11 of the Director-General's Report were not exhaustive and therefore should not limit the discussion. Consequently, the discussion ought to include other questions which were just as important. The Workers also underlined the fact that consideration of the problem should not be restricted by the conclusions of the Tripartite Advisory Meeting held in May 1976. Under these circumstances, the three international trade union federations asked that, on the international and national levels, steps should be taken to strengthen control of multinational enterprises. This control should be exerted by the countries in which they operated. The areas in which international and national action should take place were, in particular, as follows:

(i) in all the countries where multinational enterprises operated, the existing Conventions of the ILO ought to be applied, in particular Conventions Nos. 87 on trade union liberties, 98 on collective bargaining, 100 on equal remuneration, 122 on employment, 135 on representation of workers, 140 on paid education leave and 143 on migrant workers. In addition, reference to ILO Conventions must include working conditions for multinational enterprises in countries which had not yet ratified these ILO standards and in those countries where they were persistently violated;

(ii) employment of local workers and non-discrimination should be guaranteed. Non-discriminatory working conditions should be established on a democratic basis and should correspond to the highest wages, salaries, working conditions and standards of hygiene and safety in all the branches and units of multinational enterprises;

(iii) multinational enterprises ought to guarantee that the enterprises supply the representatives of the workers with essential information, especially on the composition of capital, the general organisation of the company at the level of the parent company and the branches, the evolution of the company with respect to workers' participation, detailed investment plans, current and former agreements, conditions of work, wages and recruitment of personnel in each factory, data on financial management and results, etc.;

(iv) in addition, the right of trade unions to take solidarity action at the level of each factory and of the multinational organisation as a whole, and the right of trade unions to decide freely on any action designed to enforce economic sanctions;

(v) the transfer of activities following labour conflicts should be prohibited. In the case of a transfer of production, workers should be provided with new jobs with equivalent working conditions, and a compensation fund should be created to support workers losing their jobs;

(vi) furthermore, in a more general economic context, the profits of multinational enterprises should remain in the countries in which these enterprises operated in order to contribute to the creation of productive employment and to a healthier balance of payments situation.

111. The Workers' members felt that in order to achieve this, several convergent paths should be followed at both national and international levels. On the one hand, it would be desirable to strengthen legislative and executive powers to provide the possibility of prohibiting certain economic concentrations, to integrate the activities of the companies in national planning and to provide for real public control over exchange, prices, monetary movements, investments, taxation and credit. On the other hand, the sovereign rights of States to nationalise in order to control their development and their sovereignty over natural resources should be respected. The right to nationalise should apply particularly when the interests of the workers or the country were threatened. Finally, it was necessary that a code of conduct should be elaborated at the international level defining the obligations of multinational enterprises. This code should take into account notably the principles and measures presented by the Workers' members. It should have a legal and binding form.

112. The Workers' members recognised the importance of the principle of non-discrimination between multinational enterprises and national companies in industrialised countries, but stressed that the very nature of multinational companies and the problems relating to them necessitated the possibility of making exceptions to this principle. In developing countries it was permissible and in some cases even necessary, in the interest of the development of these countries, to take measures which were discriminatory.

113. All foreign investments should be undertaken under the general conditions set out in paragraphs 110-112 and 114. In this context the multinational corporations should abide by the following principles:

(i) local subcontracting when this is technically possible;

(ii) a progressive increase in the local processing of raw materials;

(iii) local reinvestment of profits to the greatest extent possible;

(iv) replacement of expatriates and maximum utilisation of local personnel;

(v) training and promotion of local production workers and of local management personnel;

(vi) co-operation on matters of training with the various local institutions providing training.

114. Multinational enterprises should be required to study the manner in which they could adapt the activities of their subsidiaries to the development

programmes and economic objectives of the countries where they were established. The multinational enterprises must respect the sovereign rights of States and take into consideration the legislation, regulations and relevant national practices as well as internationally recognised obligations. They must also recognise the rights of workers and should not undermine but contribute to progress in the field of standards and conditions of work in the host country.

115. As to future action of the ILO, a majority of the Workers' members insisted on the need to strengthen the technical capacity of developing countries to negotiate with multinational enterprises. In this field it was desirable that the ILO, to the extent of its competence, should be ready to provide the required technical assistance to governments desiring to strengthen their bargaining power vis-à-vis multinational enterprises.

116. A large number of the Workers' members thought that it would also be desirable to request the ILO to carry out studies on policies concerning employment, training and wages followed by developing countries in relation to multinational enterprises. It would also be desirable to step up research in the field of appropriate technology and on products with a high employment content, the production of which it would be desirable to promote in the developing countries. For their part the multinational enterprises, so far as possible, should devote themselves to stepping up research and development in the field of appropriate technology and the development of products for furthering employment creation.

117. The Workers' members stressed that the ILO should deal with all the areas relating to the social aspects of the activities of multinational enterprises. The work of the ILO in these fields should be closely co-ordinated with the activities of the UN Commission on Transnational Corporations.

118. The Workers' members finally considered that:

(i) the ILO should continue its current work concerning multinationals and social policy on the basis of the conclusions of the Tripartite Advisory Meeting of 4-12 May 1976, but without confining itself to those conclusions;

(ii) the ILO should contribute in the field of its competence and within the United Nations to the elaboration of an international instrument (Code of Conduct) with a binding character permitting the control of multinational companies;

(iii) the ILO, within the framework of a reform of the mechanisms for examining questions concerning the violation of trade union freedom, should provide for a procedure to be applied to multinational corporations;

(iv) the ILO Governing Body should at its next meeting give consideration to the respective positions of the governments, the Employers' group and the Workers' group at the World Employment Conference;

(v) the ILO Governing Body should place the issue of multinational enterprises and social policy on the agenda of the 1978 Session of the International Labour Conference, in order that Conventions on multinational enterprises should be adopted in the following areas: industrial relations, training for employment, conditions of life and work.

119. The Workers' members expressed their profound dissatisfaction that it was not possible to reach any common points of agreement on this crucially important subject. They moreover wished to point out in this context that a number of individual points of agreement were recorded between the Workers' members and several governments. The Workers' members expressed their support for the proposals of the Group of 77, in particular the basic principles covered by paragraph 85. They also supported points (i)—(vi) in paragraph 92 as proposed by the Government members of industrialised market economy countries.

APPENDIX. STATEMENTS CONCERNING THE DECLARATION OF PRINCIPLES AND THE PROGRAMME OF ACTION

Statement by the Government delegate of Luxembourg on behalf of the member States of the European Community

(Translation)

I would like to make a statement on behalf of the European Community and its member States.

We are very grateful for the efforts which have gone into the production of the Declaration of Principles and of the Programme of Action which we are considering. In particular, Mr. President, we are appreciative of the contribution made by the Chairman of the Committee of the Whole, Dr. Subroto of Indonesia.

The Governments for which I speak wish to emphasis their support for the "basic needs" approach. The result of our work constitutes a compromise which includes for everyone, as the discussion in the Committee of the Whole demonstrated, some acceptable elements and some unacceptable elements. Taking into account the compromise nature of the document, I am glad to be able to state that the nine members of the European Community can associate themselves with the consensus achieved on the Declaration of Principles and the Programme of Action for submission to the Governing Body of the ILO.

In thus associating themselves with the general consensus, the Community and its member States are conscious that the Declaration of Principles and the Programme of Action are wide-ranging and ambitious and that they contain proposals of concern to many international bodies. In so far as these proposals fall within the competence of the ILO, we accept that they will be considered by the Governing Body and we hope that the programmes of the ILO will in large measure take them into account. In so far as the proposals fall within the competence of other UN bodies or international organisations, the European Community and the Governments for which I speak wish to emphasise that their views on many of these issues have been made clear in other fora, most recently in the course of UNCTAD IV. The European Community and its member States approved important resolutions in Nairobi and confirm that they stand ready to implement them. At the same time, the fact that they are associating themselves with the consensus achieved today does not of itself imply acceptance of proposals going beyond those resolutions.

Moreover, Mr. President, it goes without saying that nothing in this document can affect existing international agreements or can be invoked in order to weaken them.

Finally, Mr. President, we hope that the work begun at this Conference will be followed up within the ILO and other appropriate bodies. We are confident that this Conference will be considered as having made an important contribution to world-wide employment strategies.

Statement by the Government delegate of Switzerland

(Translation)

By participating in the consensus by which the text was adopted by the Conference, the Government delegation of Switzerland wished to demonstrate its comprehension and its support for the preoccupations of the developing countries with problems of employment and more particularly underemployment.

In connection with the references to the ratification of certain ILO Conventions, the Swiss Government delegation wishes, however, to recall that the autonomy of the competent authorities of States must be respected, in conformity with the Constitution of the Organisation.

Regarding the points in the text which fall within the field of responsibility of other international organisations, particularly UNCTAD and GATT, Switzerland's participation in the consensus implies no change in the positions which it took in these organisations on the subjects in question, and most recently at the Fourth Session of UNCTAD.

Letter of 18 June 1976 from the Ambassador and Permanent Representative of Mexico to the Director-General

(Translation)

Sir,

I have the honour to refer to the statement made by the Chairman of the Group of 77 at the closing sitting of the Tripartite World Conference on Employment, Income Distribution and Social Progress, and the International Division of Labour.

I hereby inform you that, in conformity with the above-mentioned statement, my Government has decided to request you to arrange for official publication of the following reservation in the appropriate section of the Final Record.

"The Government delegation of Mexico to the Tripartite World Conference on Employment, Income Distribution and Social Progress, and the International Division of Labour reserves the position of its Government with regard to paragraph 18 of the Declaration of Principles adopted by the Conference, the text of which is as follows:

'NOTING the firm commitment of the developing countries and of some developed countries to implement the New International Economic Order, based on the principles contained in the Charter of Economic Rights and Duties of States;'.

The Government delegation of Mexico refrained from submitting amendments to this Declaration of Principles—notably with respect to the paragraph quoted—in view of the fact that the final stages of parliamentary debate required that all delegations should refrain from formulating suggested texts or submitting amendments in order that a consensus should be reached on the Declaration of Principles and in order to avoid the submission of a large number of amendments which would have had the effect of preventing the adoption of any document.

For this reason the spokesman of the Group of 77, speaking on behalf of the Group, made it clear that the Governments which were members of the Group reserved their right to express their reservations once the Declaration of Principles and Programme of Action of the Conference had been approved.

The Government delegation of Mexico wishes to state, subject to any position which the Governments belonging to the Group of 77 might adopt on this question, that in its opinion the resolutions adopted by international bodies in accordance with their constitutional provisions are applicable not only to the countries which vote in their favour but to all the members of the organisation in which they are adopted especially where such resolutions enshrine standards of conduct covering the activity of the international community as a whole, as is the case of the Charter of Economic Rights and Duties of States.

The suggestion that standards of conduct which should be followed by all States which are members of the international community only govern the conduct of those States which supported them is equivalent to a denial of the existence of an organised international community and amounts to an incitement to anarchy at the international level.

The Government delegation of Mexico cannot support the implication in the paragraph in question that the New International Economic Order applies only to the developing countries and to some developed countries, particularly in view of the fact that the General Assembly of the United Nations, at its Seventh Special Session, recognised by consensus that the Charter of Economic Rights and

Duties of States lays down the foundations of the New International Economic Order; that it should be the basis of greater co-operation among States to contribute to strengthening peace and security in the world: and that the economic and social system of the United Nations should be more responsive to the requirements of its provisions."

I should be grateful for your prompt attention to this request which I am making on the instructions of my Government.

I have the honour to be,
Yours, etc.

(signed)
Manuel Armendáriz,
Ambassador,
Permanent Representative.

Letter of 22 July 1976 from the United States Ambassador to the Director-General

Dear Mr. Director-General:

The United States Government wishes to confirm the following reservations it took during the World Employment Conference on the final document (WEC/CW/E.1).

1. In general, the United States reserves position on any part of the final document that could be construed to indicate a deviation from positions taken by the United States at the Sixth and Seventh Special Sessions of the General Assembly and UNCTAD IV.

2. The United States agrees fully with the reservation of western industrialised countries expressed in paragraph 26.

3. Along with "most western industrialised countries", the United States does not support the establishment of a Consultative Group on Appropriate Technology and an International Appropriate Technology Unit, as indicated in paragraph 62, for the reasons stated in the United States delegate's speech to the Committee of the Whole on June 9 and by the Government representative in Working Group III.

Sincerely,

(signed)
Francis L. Dale
Ambassador.